CW00539717

Francis of Assisi

Francis of Assisi

Paintings for our Time

Paintings & Stone Carvings
Greg Tricker

Introduction
Jeremy Naydler

Historical Background
Johannes Steuck

Green Books

Greg Tricker's paintings are represented by

PIANONOBILE
FINE PAINTINGS

129 PORTLAND ROAD
LONDON W11 4LW
Tel/fax: 020 7229 1099
art@piano-nobile.com

Johannes Steuck would like to dedicate his
Historical Background to the life of St Francis
to Heidi Steffen and Andy Benham.

Published in 2005 by
Green Books, Foxhole, Dartington, Totnes, Devon TQ9 6EB
www.greenbooks.co.uk

Book designed with illustrated drop caps by Greg Tricker

The stories that complement each of the plates on pages 31-141
were collated by Greg Tricker with reference to the original
source material as outlined in the bibliography.

Printed in Slovenia on paper made from 50% recycled pulp.

ISBN 1 903998 66 2

St Francis • The Draper Shop

Francis & The Poor Woman

Contents

List of Plates

Journey to Assisi

By Greg Tricker

BY THE MILLWHEEL, a yellow wagtail glides across the cascading waterfall that flows foaming white over the olive green mosses below. There is a great roaring sound of water falling. A fine misty spray rises up, and drifts across to where I stone-carve a huge slab of shelly Cotswold limestone. The rhythmic sound of the stone-hammer striking the metal chisel rings out, echoing across the valley. As I carve, the light hits the chiselled surface of the stone, shaping and forming at the cutting edge. Here is a threshold, a possibility point, between what becomes broken and discarded, and a discovery that brings a sense of purpose, shapes reality. Working with the simple rough stone, I sense a sharpening awareness that brings me closer to the spirit.

A mood of expectancy fills the air. Suddenly I feel a sense of wonder and joy as I see emerging in the sculpted stone the humble, kind face of St Francis with a fiery beard and a long shelly sack-cloth tunic. Then, uncovering more, I discover the fossilised hands of St Francis touching the wings of Sister Bird. He holds a universe close. The carving completed, 'freed from the stone', I felt inspired to paint, as if I was being handed down buckets of fire from above, that I must pass on. The first painting was on wood; a glorious yellow sun rising above a kneeling St Francis, full of joy, holding a white dove. Then, painting on hessian sackcloth, the feeling of St Francis and Lady Poverty deepened. Quietly listening, 'seeing' into the material sackcloth and grainy wood, I could sense their arrival, the forming and shaping of each detail.

A feeling of companionship and closeness to St Francis was growing. While I walked by the river, St Francis seemed to be nearby, in the tall swaying rushes growing wild. I sensed a journey unfolding, an inner quest to discover more deeply the mystery; the world of St Francis. I must go to Assisi. I travelled to Italy, passing through Bologna and Florence to arrive by train in Assisi.

A deep autumn mist was rising up from the plain of Spoleto and drifting up the mountainous hills around Assisi, lingering on the olive groves and in the medieval streets. Climbing up the granite steps that wind upwards, I pass Gothic stone-arched doorways with studded oaken doors. I hear a distant bell ring. The narrow cobbled street begins to rise steeply. High above me washing hangs down by shuttered windows, where Italian women lean out, laughing and shouting across to each other. I pass under a huge archway into a quiet alleyway that leads onto a courtyard with large pebbled stones. I look up, surprised to see the name of St Francis inscribed on a lintel above a door. This was the home, the stable-like birthplace of St Francis. The tall wooden doors swinging on the old metal hinges are slightly open. I peek inside. Through the darkness I can see a bench along an arched wall, and a mysterious gilded painting of St Francis in the corner. I sit on a bench, and enter into a profound, peaceful silence. In the silence there seems to echo a feeling of the original Bethlehem stable with the Christ child.

Leaving the courtyard, I climb more stone steps and pass under a low domed archway. Then unexpectedly the street opens out into a magnificent square, 'Piazza del Comune', with high-rising Corinthian columns of the ancient Roman Forum, the temple of the Goddess, Minerva, dated 1st century BC. A crowd gathers around a street trader with puppets jumping to organ music, while people are talking at tables, with glasses of wine. A bell rings loudly from a tower above, as a fountain cascades into a bath-bowl where birds are merrily splashing, preening themselves. I rest my bag, which drops onto the pinky marble stones. Suddenly all the birds rise up, flying around the square. Seeing them fly so swiftly, while moving so miraculously together, a feeling of divine harmony fills the air. The presence of ragged St Francis seems near, as if he were also in the square looking upwards, smiling and talking to the birds.

FURTHER on I pass San Rufino Cathedral, with its beautiful Romanesque façade, and walk across the walled-in square where St Francis preached to the crowds of both poor and noble people. Leaving the town I go deeper into the countryside, down sloping hills, and follow a dusty winding road that leads to the small church of San Damiano, rebuilt by St Francis. The light streams into the chapel through a rounded doorway. I enter into the quiet, humble chapel. I am standing in a sacred space, on the stones where St Francis knelt to pray; eyes lifted to the crucifix above. It was here that he received the revelation of Christ that transformed his life and threw light into the world. I stay a while at the back of the chapel on a pew, silently drawing. Later, going further into the chapel down winding steps, I enter the choir room of St Clare, where the 'Poor Clares' would be singing at day break, or in prayer, living a life of poverty and contemplation.

Leaving San Damiano, I explore further into the hilly terrain and wild fields. I find a small olive grove. The gnarled twisted olive trees grow amongst the stony ledges where playful butterflies dance between the grasses, cornflowers and crickets; a timeless Eden where nature still bathes in a joyous jubilant light. This is the world of St Francis. I stop to ponder for a moment upon the vision of St Francis. He holds a unique perception, an all-embracing passion for life and a way of seeing the world anew. A world of brotherhood. St Francis reaches across, beyond so-called religion, to lepers and the poor. He reaches across pain and freezing cold weather with frosty hands to touch the first spring flowers which speak of beauty and the divine world. He reaches the heart. Seeing the sacred in all things; in stars, flowers, crickets, lepers, the sun, moon and the bees, St Francis truly reached 'the spirit of each being'. He reached the spirit in me.

Introduction

By Jeremy Naydler

HROUGH THE AGES St Francis has been portrayed many times by artists. Greg Tricker has produced a new image of Francis for our own age. As much as these pictures are an outpouring of creativity, they are a response of the artist to an equal inpouring of inspiration. At first glance, the pictures reproduced in this book appear simply to be illustrations of various episodes in the life of St Francis of Assisi. To describe them in this way, however, would be to do them an injustice. While they each bring to us a vivid portrayal of a more or less familiar incident in the life of Francis, they do much more than this. For they also portray depths of human suffering and exultation, compassion and celebration, that stand behind these incidents in the saint's life, without which the incidents themselves would not have taken place. In these pictures, we are led to 'see through' the stories of St Francis to the archetype of human sanctity or sainthood that Francis embodied. In this respect these works of art have a truly visionary quality, for they reach into and represent for us a condition of 'being human' in which the human coalesces with the divine.

These images, then, are only peripherally about the life of St Francis. At a deeper and more subtle level, they are about an inner quality of soul that we may arrive at only when we have stripped away the veneer of culture and sophistication with which we all habitually clothe ourselves, and which we are inclined to regard as perfectly normal, even essential for a decent quality of life. Yet to look at, for example, the image of Francis reaching with such passionate intensity toward a snowdrop (see *Francis in the Snow*), or to see his forthrightly loving embrace of a leper (see *Francis with the Leper*), is to see that a far deeper and far more essential quality of life is being represented in these pictures. Francis's life-path, his career, makes absolutely no sense in the eyes of 'the world'. He lived a kind of inverse life, deliberately renouncing the values to which we all in varying degrees subscribe, and to which most of us aspire. From the dramatic event of his stripping himself naked in the town square, in front of his father, the priest and gathered townsfolk, renouncing the prosperous career so carefully prepared for him, everything he did was counter to common sense, counter to what reasonable people do (see *The Trial*). We could say that Francis was an extremist, but only through this extremism could he find the way to God.

Francis referred to himself as a fool, an *idiota*. He lived his life as a holy simpleton, knowing that the key to being truly human is to simplify. And he so radically simplified that he lived his life as a beggar, a vagabond who wandered from place to place with no possessions, positively avoiding both material comfort and the kind of spiritual comfort that derives from cultural and leisure activities, in particular from reading and studying books. He deliberately chose to be UNKNOWLEDGEABLE, basing his life entirely on the Gospels and his own intimate and prayerful relationship with Christ. He was deeply suspicious of books and book learning, suspicious of any kind of cleverness. His message was that we cannot come to Christ without losing our relationship to "the world"—in other words, to all those aspects of life that remove us from innocence. There is a Being of Love within each of us, to which each of us belongs in our true and original humanity. But it has become obscured by our desires for security, wealth, knowledge, and personal gain, on the one hand, and our endless anxieties and lack of trust in the universe on the other. All too easily we allow ourselves to be drawn away from the root of our humanity, which we can only come near to when we simplify.

Today we hear a great deal about 'personal growth' and 'inner development'. But St Francis was less interested in growth and development than in SHEDDING, in becoming simple, and thereby coming into contact with a purity of feeling and impulse that issues from our original nature. For Francis this original nature is innately good. If he also had a profound awareness of his own sinfulness, this should really be understood as an awareness of the degree to which he felt distanced from his essential humanity.

Francis lived a fundamental truth, a hard, almost impossible truth for us today, because the tenor of our culture is so unremittingly secular. He understood that practically everything we tend to think of as normal and necessary for living takes us away from the central core of our humanity. And at the core of our humanity, he knew there is the Being of Love, the Christ.

F only we could 'simply be' human, then we would of necessity at the same time 'be loving'. For that is our true nature. Hence his total dedication to simplicity, or, as he put it, to Lady Poverty. If the requirement that Francis placed on himself and those who followed his way was to simplify, then this was not without its paradox. One might think that he and the brothers would have become rather boringly similar to each other. But the opposite in fact happened. Simplification meant that his and the brothers' eccentricities became all the more accentuated. As if our individual character traits are amplified by losing the social graces that so effectively work against our being truly ourselves. A childlike enthusiasm replaces adult reserve. This is beautifully illustrated in the accounts that have come down to us of how Francis used to take up a stick to play an imaginary viol while singing with reckless joy (see *Francis with Viol*). How touching that he and his companions called themselves 'the minstrels of God', but didn't possess a single instrument between them.

Instead of 'spiritual maturity', a more apt phrase to describe St Francis's inner state would be 'spiritual childhood'. It was said of Francis in his own day that you couldn't see him without loving him. It was as if he had become profoundly innocent in his whole being. How does one become so thoroughly innocent? Not by acquiring more knowledge, more subtlety of understanding, more clever insights, more of anything that bolsters up the self, but rather by losing all of that and devoting oneself to Lady Poverty.

It is worth dwelling a little on this unusual feminine archetype to whom Francis devoted himself so unreservedly. Europe, in our times, is characterised by overflowing wealth, an overabundance of material goods that enables us to live lifestyles that would have been the envy of many a medieval king. At the same time modern culture is driven by a kind of terror of poverty. We legislate against it, we launch social campaigns against it, we throw up our hands in horror at it and expend great efforts to protect everyone from it, and yet Francis devoted himself to it. Like a gallant knight, he vowed to serve Lady Poverty as his ideal above all others.

Of all the images in this marvellous collection, it is those that show Francis holding a dove to his heart, that symbolise most exactly the meaning of his relationship to his Lady (see *St Francis and the Dove*, *Brother Sun*, *St Francis Sun and Moon*). The dove is, significantly, not only a Christian image of the Holy Spirit but also an age-old symbol of the ancient goddesses of love, from the Sumerian Inanna to Atargatis, Ishtar and Aphrodite. Francis knew that devotion to material and spiritual poverty leads to a kind of inner softening and gentleness. And this inner softening and gentleness involves an opening of the heart, through which the lost feminine is reinstated within Christianity. It is this that accounts for the extraordinary appeal of St Francis. Instead of knowledge, power or material wealth, his concern is with relationship, compassion and love—inner 'feminine' qualities that cannot flourish except in the soul that has become simplified through poverty.

Most of the pictures in this collection show Francis in relationship—in relationship to plants, to animals, to rocks and soil, to other human beings, to monks and lepers, and also to spiritual beings whom he saw in his visions. These latter are not always beneficent (see *Meeting the Demons*). Francis suffered terrible inner torment, just as he suffered most of his life from physical sickness, but these were both part of his discipline of dedication to Lady Poverty. His gesture toward all that he experienced was to embrace it as his 'sister' or 'brother', thereby entering into a heartfelt relationship with it—even in the end with 'sister death'. It is this quality of full and open-hearted relationship to everything and everyone that he encountered that reveals in Francis an ever stronger fundamental relationship to and identity with the Being of Love, the Christ.

RANCIS was a man who was possessed by Christ. Especially towards the end of his life, people felt that they were no longer just in the presence of the saint, but of the Christ in him. This is why he inspired such love. This may also account for the reactions of animals to Francis. They did not fear him because, like them, he had become totally simple and at one with his own intrinsic nature. But more than that, the being he had become one with was the Being of Love, and this in their innocence they could implicitly trust. In the representations of St Francis gathered together in this collection, we

cannot help but be struck by the extraordinary harmony between the style of painting and its subject matter. If these images were any more sophisticated, they would lose this harmony. They need to be simple, they need to have an innocence, a kind of naivety, and gentle humour in order to capture the simplicity, innocence and sweetness of their subject. The authentically Franciscan spirit of these paintings leaves us in no doubt as to the genuineness of their inspirational source. I have several times been privileged to visit the studio where they were brought into the world. It is a crudely constructed shed perched on the side of a steep hill in the heart of England, surrounded by trees and overlooking a beautiful lake. Its atmosphere is more of a sanctuary, a hermitage, than a studio. Going inside, one immediately feels that in its simplicity and 'poverty', this is a place inwardly open to the invisible. Here the artist opens a window to the transcendent, is blessed with visions and is empowered to translate them into radiant images.

St Francis of Assisi

Historical Background by Johannes Steuck

A CHRISTIANITY without St Francis would be unimaginably poorer and bleaker. He appears like a burning meteor, illuminating for a while the corrupt world. He lived life out of the fullness of Christ; a fresh new morning of faith, giving hope to a tired humanity. He appeared at a time when the Middle Ages were in full flower. There was still much strife and bloodshed, but enough stability for the development of religious and secular culture.

Both Notre Dame Cathedral and Chartres were under construction in his lifetime. Notre Dame was begun in 1163 and consecrated in 1235. Chartres, which became the greatest school of mediæval scholasticism, was begun in 1160 and consecrated in 1260.

Wolfram von Eschenbach was born in 1172 and wrote his Parzival story in 1203. It gives us a window into an otherwise dark period of history (the 9th century) and describes the hidden stream of Grail Christianity.

The golden thread of Christian esotericism was passed on to the Knights Templar founded in Jerusalem in 1118. They united the vows of monkhood with chivalry and tried to embody a true Christianity in their absolute devotion to the resurrected Christ.

In a great outpouring of confident, barbarous European energy, Jerusalem had been conquered by the Frankish armies of the first crusade in 1099. Saladin recaptured it in 1187, five years after the birth of Francis in 1182.

Innocent III became Pontiff in 1198, reigning till 1216. He was a strong prince of the Church who managed to gain authority over most of the European kings and win back territory formerly under papal control. A kind of balance of power was temporarily established between the spiritual and secular, between Church and State.

A reaction had set in against the worldly power of the Church, both within it and outside it. Ragged preaching friars travelled the lands and the great heresies of the Albigensians and Waldensians had wide influence. The Albigensian or Catharist heresy, influenced by Manicheism, had many adherents in the Languedoc province of France. It was brutally crushed and an alternative shoot of Christianity lopped off. Through the life and work of St Francis, strong spiritual currents which had existed only outside the Church could once again enliven it from within.

His Life

ST Francis was born in Assisi in 1182. His mother, the Lady Pica, came from Provence. French language and culture were to have a profound influence on him. The songs of the Troubadours created a kind of universal culture as they travelled about in Europe. They expressed the entirely new ideal of romantic love, in which love for a woman was exalted to almost divine status. Francis expressed himself eloquently and poetically throughout his life, as much at home in French as in Italian.

His father, Pietro Bernadone, was a very wealthy cloth merchant who travelled regularly to France; it was here that he had met his wife. Francis was given the baptismal name Giovanni (John), but on his father's return was called Francesco after the country he so much admired.

As a child of a wealthy family, Francis grew up spoilt and indulged, though of nouveau-riche merchant stock; he mingled with the nobility. As a youth he seems to have been the centre of fun and merriment and often bore the title 'King of Feasts'. This was of course an honour; it also meant however that as King of Revelries, he had to bear the costs. He did this with generosity bordering on extravagance. This sense of enjoyment and natural leadership is an important part of his personality. He was never mean and miserly and, although

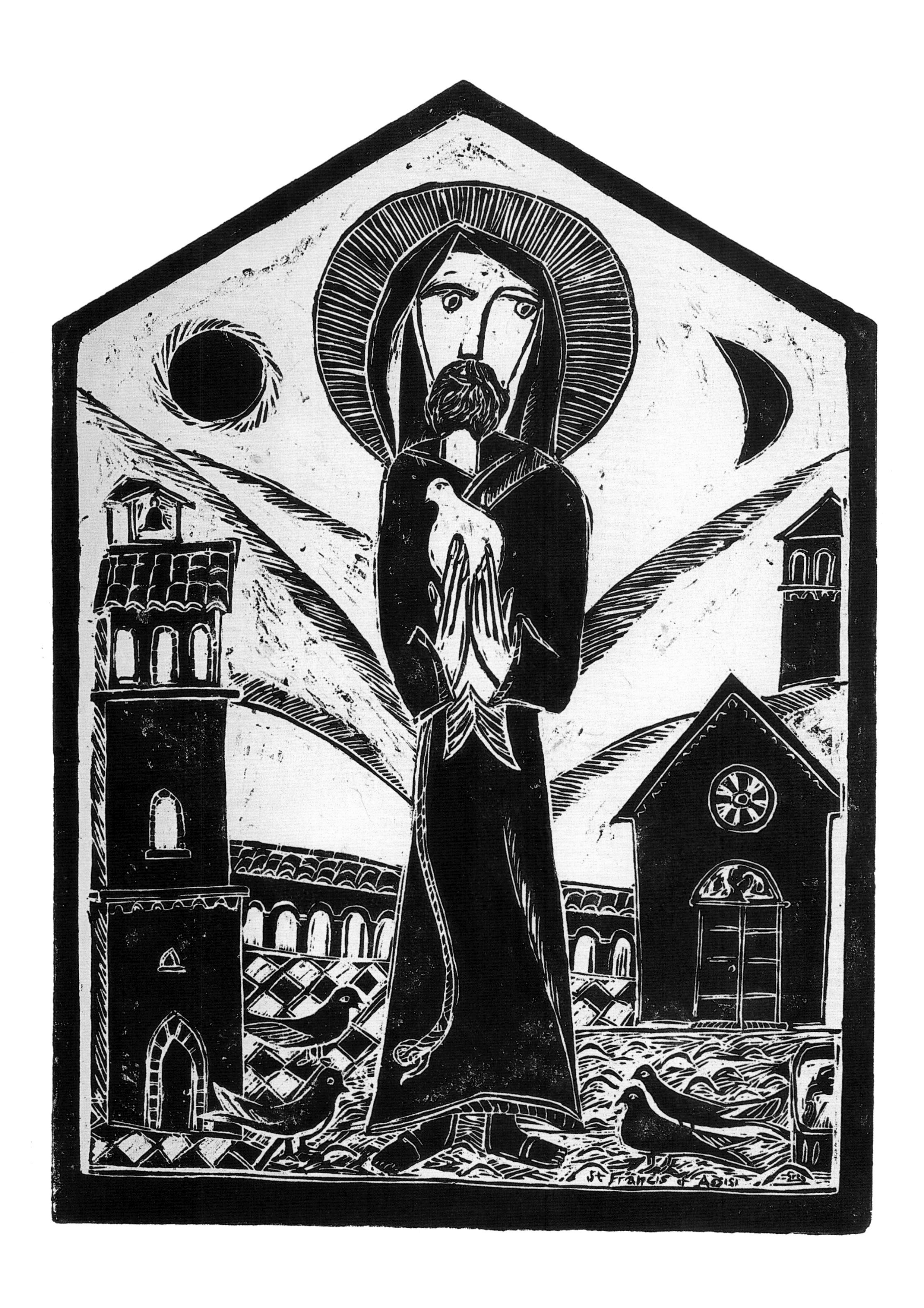

Francis, Sun & Moon

slight of body and not considered handsome, attracted everyone with his charm and charisma.

When Francis was sixteen (in 1198) a struggle broke out between the hated representatives of the Holy Roman Empire and the commune of Assisi. Overlooking the town is the menacing fortress of the Rock, a huge fortification held by the Duke of Spoleto. His position was a reward for faithful service to Henry VI. Pope Innocent III claimed the territory. Corrado of Luitzen, Duke of Spoleto, a brutal and overbearing man who had allied himself with the feudal overlords against the commune, went to surrender. He had little choice in the matter, as his master Henry VI died suddenly. In his absence, the citizens of Assisi stormed the fortress, killed the remaining garrison and began to tear it down. The stones were used to strengthen the outer walls of the town.

Carried on a wave of victory euphoria, Francis helped in carting stones and building. At this time the emerging townships saw the beginnings of a middle class. A class of people who were neither titled nor had inherited wealth—but who had created it through their own efforts, these consisted of merchants and Craftmasters (goldsmiths were the first bankers) and disaffected runaways from the feudal villages. These escapees would be free citizens if they avoided capture for a year and a day. Thus this uprising in which Francis took part was the beginning of a new era in which people felt themselves to be citizens rather than vassals.

The next conflict was less successful. Three years later, 1202, a comparatively small army of Assisians fought against Perugia, Assisi's sister city, a town some fifteen miles distant. Francis, like most young men of the time, wanted to be a knight and took part in the battle. The Assisians were crushingly defeated and the survivors, who included Francis, were clapped into a dungeon where they languished for a year, awaiting a ransom payment. The exiled nobility, which had taken refuge in Perugia, went back to Assisi.

Francis returned home, resuming his former life in the bright and sparkling circle of his pleasure-seeking friends, but perhaps his stay in a dark and rat-infested dungeon was beginning to work a change. We know that he became very ill with a high fever, and that he nearly died. Still cherishing his dreams of knighthood, he decided to leave Assisi and become the groom of an Assisian nobleman and go off to the wars. His doting father spared no expense in providing him with superb armour, weapons and a horse. The day before he was supposed to leave he met a poor knight and, in one of those impulsive, unconditionally generous gestures, gave away all his equipment. Quickly and probably without a grudge, his father re-equipped him.

IN the night Francis dreamed that he was shown a huge armoury filled with weapons, shields and flags all of pure white emblazoned with a blood-red cross. He heard a voice which said: "Francis, all these are for thee and thy soldiers." The knights and their grooms left the following morning. But Francis was not destined for a life of warfare. That very night in camp at Spoleto, he had another dream. Once again he heard the mysterious voice and it said: "Francis, who can do more for you, the lord or the servant?" "The lord," he answered. Then the voice said: "Therefore, why do you leave the lord for the servant and the prince for the vassal?" "O, Lord, what do you wish me to do?" Francis asked. "Return to Assisi and what you are to do will be revealed to you there."

This return without a single battle or the glorious accolade of knighthood must have seemed strange to his parents and friends. Yet this is very much part of his challenge—to return, not to do the expected, to face mocking laughter, misunderstanding and derision. How much easier would it have been to disappear, perhaps come back much, much later transformed with the authority of holiness. But this was not to be. Francis was rooted in Assisi; always he had to return to his old familiar ground.

He was now in his early twenties, still leading the carefree life with his former companions but perhaps a little more introspective, going off alone, praying and waiting. He had two germinal encounters. One was with a poor man whom he helped and clothed, the other with a leper.

He was riding through the countryside one day (near the leper hospital of Santa Maria Magdalena) when he saw the unmistakable figure of a leper. His noble senses were revolted; he could hardly bring himself to look at the man. But then suddenly his deep horror and revulsion were changed into an equally deep love and compassion. He realised in an instant that this utterly ill and degraded figure was his brother in Christ. Francis dismounted, embraced and kissed the astonished man.

Leprosy was the scourge of the Middle Ages, a kind of living death, mysterious and terrible, that destined its sufferers to a life of exclusion and banishment. Lepers were taken outside the city gates, prayers for the dead were intoned for them and after earth (symbolising burial) had been sprinkled over their heads they were severed from all further contact with their fellows. This process went so far that their names were struck from all registers and never spoken again. Francis's embrace of a leper was the first step on the long road of reconciliation. The care of lepers became one of his life's tasks.

Seeking solitude and stillness, Francis went to the ruined church of San Damiano to pray. There he would prostrate himself before the crucifix—a crucifix which did not so much show Christ nailed to the cross as stretching out his arms in a wide gesture of blessing which seemed to encompass the whole world. Then one day a voice spoke from the wooden cross saying,

O, Francis, and repair my house because it is falling into ruin." Full of fear and wonder he dashed off home and in a zealous and impulsive fit took some bundles of very costly silk from his father's shop. He sold them well below their true value and gave the proceeds to the old priest of San Damiano to repair the building. The old man seemed to have been acquainted with Pietro Bernadone's temper and feared to take the money, thus it remained unused on a ledge.

Francis's father was stirred to anger and the young man was locked up in the cellar at home in the hope that he would come to his senses. Lady Pica, who probably intuited something of her son's future mission, released him. Francis went back to the little ruined church and put himself under ecclesiastical jurisdiction. In October 1207 father and son went to the Episcopal court in the tiny plaza in front of the bishopric. Bernadone demanded that his son make public amends, that he renounce all hereditary rights and that he be banished from the commune according to the law. In a typically dramatic and flamboyant gesture, Francis not only gave back the money, but threw all his clothes at the feet of his father saying:

"Hear ye all, and understand. Until now I have called Pietro Bernadone my father; now I give back all that I had of him, desiring to say only 'Our Father which art in Heaven', with whom I have laid up my whole treasure and on whom I have set my whole trust and hope." Bishop Guido discreetly covered the naked youth with his mantle as the townsfolk wept with emotion. Free and happy, Francis donned a simple grey habit upon which he chalked a cross. He returned to the little church of San Damiano and began the task of repairing it. He realised that taking the money from his wealthy father was not the answer; he must rebuild it with his own hands. He begged stones and probably help from the townsfolk and not only repaired the church of San Damiano, but also that of San Pietro and of Santa Maria degli Angeli.

On his hunts for stone and begging forays into Assisi, Francis sometimes met his father. These encounters provoked Pietro's Latin temper and he would deride and curse his son. A father's curse could not be endured lightly, so Francis made a bargain with a beggar: to say prayers and make the sign of a cross over him each time his father's maledictions fell, in exchange for an equal share of begged food. It is hoped that Pietro lived long enough to appreciate his son's mission of holiness and love.

Francis took hold of his life's task through tough physical labour. He sang joyfully as he worked, happy in the new-found freedom that abandonment to God's will had bestowed. Yet, as it had not been his destiny to be a knight, he was also not fated to be God's stone mason.

One Sunday morning in February of 1208, whilst hearing mass in the tiny church of Santa Maria degli Angeli, his life's task flashed powerfully into the depths of his soul. In a state of ecstasy he heard as it were for the first time the words from Chapter 9 of St Luke's Gospel: "Provide neither gold nor silver nor brass in your purses, nor scrip for your journey, neither two coats, neither shoes nor yet staves. And as ye go, preach, saying the kingdom of Heaven is at hand." In that moment he had a revelation of absolute divine poverty: he realised that every possession, every prop and every outer security is an obstacle on the road to God. He understood that renewal, a rebirth of the true spirit of Christianity, could only be through poverty; faith in things diminished faith in God.

Legend has it that just before his birth his mother was moved (by angelic promptings) to retire into a neighbouring stable and that Francis, like Jesus himself, was born in a cattle shed. At his death he wished to be stripped of his ragged garment so that he would die naked, owning nothing, as he had come into the world.

OVERTY for Francis was not just a rejection of ownership—a non-attachment to things; it was a living reality. Poverty had the form of a being—Lady Poverty whose hand he and his followers took in order to make the long and arduous journey to Christ. *The Little Flowers of St Francis*, by Leo of Assisi and St Bonaventura, give us a vivid example of this condition of absolute poverty. A poor women begs alms at the Franciscan settlement (in the early days made of woven twigs and wattle) and the brothers have absolutely nothing to give her. So she is given a gospel. In those days books were incredibly valuable, printing did not yet exist and every letter had to be carefully written out by hand by a scribe monk. Francis so strongly believed that they were living according to the true and living gospel, that a mere 'book' could be given away to a beggar woman without regret.

In mediæval times the religious orders had immense wealth—each monk and nun was poor but they lived in the security of collective wealth. They did not need to have uncompromising faith in God because whether they were devout, hard-working, secretly sinful or non-believing, their lives still unrolled in predictable security. It was easy for a faith in God to be replaced by a faith in the church, a faith in institutions. Francis re-established the possibility of a direct and uncompromising faith in God. No institutions, no cushioning church security; the divine God-given nature of existence could be re-experienced.

A kind of 'inner paradise' could be achieved where humanity could once again taste the fruits of heaven, be directly linked to the spiritual world and be sustained by it. This condition of inner paradise was mirrored by the most abject poverty and material deprivation, sometimes involving almost unimaginable physical suffering. Francis stripped himself of his few remaining wretched things and took up his abode near the church of Santa Maria degli Angeli, the Portiuncula, so called after the tiny parcel of land that surrounds it. This cradle of the Franciscan order never belonged to the friars. It remained the property of the Benedictine Abbot of Mount Subasio. A symbolic rent of one basket of fish was given annually.

Filled with the inspiration of this new revelation, Francis preached both in Assisi and the surrounding countryside. Very soon the people's contempt and derision turned to amazement and devotion. Soon he had followers and, as in all reform movements and revolutions, it was the wealthy and educated who formed the vanguard. At the beginning, like Christ himself, he had twelve disciples: Bernard of Quintavalle, Pietro Caltani, Giles, Sabbatino, Mortico, John of Cappella, Philip the Long, John of San Costanzo, Barbaro, Bernardo, Angelo Tancredi of Rieli and Silvester.

The local bishop Guido, a long time friend of Francis, confirmed the order—the Pope had yet to do so. Thus it was decided that Francis and his little band of followers should make the journey to Rome and seek legitimacy and confirmation from the heir of St Peter. Once arrived and being unacquainted with formality and etiquette, he wandered into the papal palace. It just so chanced that the Pontiff Pope Innocent III was walking down the corridor when he came upon the intensely spiritual and intensely ragged figure of Francis.

Needless to say he had him thrown out. Yet that was not going to be the end of the matter, the young man reappeared in his dreams that very night.

NNOCENT dreamed that the great edifice of the Lateran Basilica was tottering, about to collapse. A figure approached and held it up on his shoulders; he recognised him as the beggar that he had ejected. This dream and the intervention of Cardinal Giovanni di San Paolo persuaded the Pope to confirm the Franciscan order. By confirming the Brothers Minor, the Pope was doing something very radical. The early Franciscans owned no property, indeed had no permanent dwellings. The monks lived where they could in crude huts made of mud and wattle, surrounded by quickset hedges, and worked or begged for their living.

Thus in the spring of 1210 Francis was given the tonsure, and leave to preach. Inscribed in flame, as it were, above the doorway of all religious orders were the vows of poverty, chastity and obedience. Poverty meant no or few personal possessions, chastity was a life of celibacy, a spiritual marriage to Christ, and obedience was obedience to one's superior. This chain of command stretched from the humblest parish priest right through the hierarchy of the Church to its summit, the Pope, who occupied the throne of St Peter. The Pope was seen as the living representative of God on earth. Francis never became a priest; his humility forbade him to be an authority figure. This eventually led to a crisis in the order in which established Church hierarchy sought to impose itself over the inner authority of Francis. It might be interesting to note that the Dominican Order was founded five years later in 1215.

The Dominicans and the Franciscans represent the two powerful currents of mediæval Christendom. Francis guided his followers on a path of intensified devotion; Dominic strove to spiritualise thinking. Indeed, the greatest mediæval Christian philosopher, Thomas Aquinas (1225-1274), was a son of the Order.

The Franciscan order grew and grew; it was as if after many years of hunger and thirst the true food and drink of the spirit had at last come. St Paul, in his first letter to the Corinthians, defines the nature of love. Francis defines the power of 'perfect joy'.

Perfect Joy

The Orders of St Francis

ONE DAY near Santa Maria degli Angeli, the blessed Francis called Friar Leo. "Here I am," replied the other. "Write down what is perfect joy. If a messenger should arrive from Paris announcing that all teachers of Paris had come into the Order, write down 'true joy is not therein'. If all the prelates, archbishops, bishops and even the King of France and the King of England should join the Order, write down 'true joy is not therein'. Further, if all my friars should go among the infidels and convert them all to the faith, or if I should have so much grace from God that I heal the sick and work miracles, write down 'true joy is not therein'. But what is perfect joy? I return from Perugia in the black night and I come here and it is winter, muddy and so cold that icicles form on the hem of my tunic and strike against my legs without cease and draw blood from my wounds. Thus covered with mud, soaked and frozen, I come to the door and, after I call out and knock for a long time, a friar comes and asks 'Who are you?'. I answer, 'Friar Francis'. And he says, 'Begone! This is not an hour to be wandering around!' And since I insist and knock further, he answers, 'Begone! You are a worthless fellow, a simpleton. Don't come here any more. We have just so many and have no need of you!' I still knock on the door and I say 'For the love of God, give me shelter for this night.' And he answers, 'I will not. Go to the hospital of the Cruciferi and ask there.' And if I endure all this patiently and without dismay, I say to you therefore, that therein lies perfect joy, true virtue and the salvation of the soul."

Girls who run away from home are not usually impelled to do so because they wish to become nuns. Yet this was precisely why Clare, one of the daughters of the Count of Loccorano the Ofreduici, did so. She had been aware of Francis for some time and was filled with an intense desire to follow him. Her aristocratic kinsmen tried to force her return but, on seeing her shaven head, gave up, astonished. It was all too much when Clare's sixteen-year-old younger sister, Agnes, ran away too. This time the armed men hardened their resolve and managed to drag her outside, but when miraculously her body became so fearfully heavy that it could not be lifted, they bowed to the inevitable and departed.

Thus the second order, the Order of the Nuns, was founded in 1212. They took their abode around the repaired church of San Damiano. Women in those days could not enjoy the freedoms of their male counterparts; the nuns had to live as an enclosed order within a monastery. They grew herbs for medicines, sewed garments and prayed—the community of monks supported them. Clare and Francis loved each other profoundly in so far as it is possible for two people to love each other in Christ. Theirs was the transcendent love of brother and sister souls, perhaps long known and enduring throughout eternity. Many lay people were inspired by Francis and in the midst of their busy worldly lives wished to be his followers. Thus the third order—or Order of Continents came into being. This was part of the uniquely Franciscan process; the treasures of the spirit were not only to be guarded by monks and nuns within the confines of the religious orders, they were to be shared freely with all. Lord Orlando of Chiusi in Castantino was the first lay brother. He gave the Franciscans a priceless treasure, Mount La Verna, upon whose summit the saint would one day receive the stigmata.

Members of the Third Order had to give up fighting (sometimes feuds continued through the generations) be reconciled with enemies, give back ill-gotten gains, and live in harmony with others. The Third Order inspired many illustrious men and women and was a channel through which the Franciscan inspiration could enliven cultural life. For example Giotto, the great painter of Francis's life, wore the habit. Francis was very much a bringer of peace. This striving is expressed fully in the words of his own prayer:

LORD, make me an instrument of your peace,
Where there is hatred, let me sow love,
Where there is injury, let me sow pardon,
Where there is discord, let me sow unity,
Where there is doubt, let me sow faith,
Where there is despair, let me sow hope.
Where there is sadness, let me sow joy,
Where there is darkness, let me sow light.
O Divine Master, grant that I may not so much seek
To be consoled, as to console,
To be understood, as to understand.
To be loved, as to love.
For it is in giving that we receive,
It is in pardoning that we are pardoned,
It is in dying that we are born into eternal life.

Tradition tells us that during one of his journeys Francis arrived at Trezzo, but did not enter because the city walls were swarming with demons. The inhabitants were at war with each other, and brother Silvester was sent in to make peace. He marched into the town, and like a town crier called out to the demons to depart in the name of God. They fled, and peace was restored. Friars sang and played in the streets and market places; their songs of joy and wonder had a profound effect on their listeners, moving people to deeds of reconciliation and forgiveness.

A short biographical sketch of the Saint would not be complete without a mention of his very special relationship to the natural world. The ancients did not enjoy or appreciate nature in the sense of a Wordsworth or Hopkins. They either experienced themselves as part of it or, as in the case of the Jews, apart from it. The established church had moved further and further away from nature, treating it with suspicion almost, demonising the old divine forces that stirred and moved within it. The words "And God saw that it was good", which come after every phase of creation, seemed long forgotten. The world was a fallen place, where any form of natural enjoyment was suspect. The Lateran council held in 870 was a further step to estrangement. It abolished the notion of an individualised human spirit, granting man only a soul and a body, with the occasional spirit flicker "bestowed from above". If indeed man's highest member is soul, then the rest of nature is practically lifeless (dumb and witless).

FRANCIS saw in nature, in fire and water, earth and air, sun, moon and every living thing a manifestation of God. He re-established a joyful, loving and respectful relationship to it. One can only guess with what profound emotion St Francis's dealings with the animal world were witnessed. That the wild things, snared and hunted and eaten, should have forgotten their fear and swarmed to the holy man must have seemed utterly miraculous. It may have conjured up a deeply buried memory of a time when the first man and the first woman lived in a beautiful garden surrounded by fearless creatures: a time before separation, when man and God and nature still lived within each other, when there was no shame and toil and fear, all was holy, all was perfect, all was one.

Some of his miraculous encounters with animals will be dealt with later in connection with the stories represented in Greg Tricker's paintings. Perhaps Francis's inauguration of the first Christmas crib can serve to define his relationship to divine nature in a broader sense. Francis was at Fonte Columbo, one of his retreats, for the Christmas season of 1223. He wanted to celebrate the festival in a simple and poetical manner, and thus the first crib was constructed and with it, an enactment of the world's first Christmas night.

"The day of gladness was drawing near. Friars, men, women gathered from all parts; each one, with his soul full of joy, prepared candles and torches to illumine that night which was to illumine the centuries like a glittering star. The saint of God finally arrived; he saw that everything had been prepared, and was comforted. The manger was readied; it was stocked with hay, and the ox and the little donkey were led into it. The night, as brilliant as day, was a delight to behold for men and beasts. The friars, with their candles, rendered to God the praises that were due to Him. The saint stood before the manger emitting deep sighs, gripped by devotion and in a transport of joy; the rite of mass was celebrated in the manger and the saint, who was deacon, put on the vestments of the sacred function and sang the gospel. His voice, passionate, sweet, clear and sonorous, invited those present to consider the reward of heaven. He preached to the people on the nativity of the King who became poor and on the tiny village of Bethlehem, and he found words which were as sweet as honey; often when he mentioned Jesus Christ, he burned with such ardour that he called Him the Child of Bethlehem and modulated His name like the bleating of a little lamb; the gentleness of his affection seemed to suffuse his mouth more than his voice."

Account from an eye-witness

Legend tells us that the visualisation of the crowd of worshippers was so intense that they actually 'saw' a baby in the crib. This event not only rekindled the flame of the 'inner child', a being of joy, wonder and reverence that lives within us all, but placed the baby betwixt ox and ass, those two dumb and humble serving beasts who from time immemorial have helped humanity to bear the toil of the earth. The child, lying jewel-like between these creatures, can give us an intuition of redemption, a thought perhaps that one day the animals will no longer need to serve us, but regain primeval equality of being. For Francis there was no higher and lower, no great divide between human and other, all things were equal, nothing was excluded from his reverence and love.

N 1219 he sailed for the orient, joining a new crusade that Pope Innocent III had urged on Christendom. Hope still lingered that the Holy places could be retaken and the Saracens driven out. Like so many Christians before him, Francis was inspired by missionary zeal, but perhaps also by life's crowning reward of martyrdom. It is not that he sought death; it was more that a death in imitation of Christ would bring him that much closer to Christian perfection. He was not to find death in Egypt, however, for the Sultan Malek-el-Khamil was both charmed and delighted by him. How different this poor and weaponless man must have appeared from all those bloodthirsty and uncouth hordes of the crusade!

The warlike Arabs had spread Islam by the sword, but generally showed a keen respect for civilisation and civilians. The crusaders had respected neither, destroying and plundering wherever they went, and sometimes, if the fall of Jerusalem is anything to go by, literally wading ankle-deep in blood. Francis offered to undergo a trial by fire to convince Malek of the truth, but the Sultan wisely rejected the idea. There is no conversion from Christianity or Islam. Thus Francis was forced to depart, his mission seemingly unfulfilled and his life intact. Legend tells us that Malek wished to be baptised on his deathbed and that mysteriously two friars appeared at the very moment of his passing and were ushered into the bedchamber.

Francis received a free pass to the holy places from Malek-el-Khamil's brother, Conradin. It is very likely that he journeyed to the Holy Land and bathed for a while in the aura of Christ's nearness that still clung to the land. On his return from Egypt in 1221, the Order was in crisis. It had become an enormous entity spread throughout Europe, unwieldy and sundered by factions. The reformers, headed by Brother Elias, hankered for less absolute biblical poverty, more security and worldliness; the 'Spirituals' wished to retain the initial purity of the Franciscan impulse. Exhausted, ill, and suffering from an eye affliction contracted in Egypt, Francis went to see Honorius III, Innocent's successor.

Cardinal Ugolino was appointed protector of the Order. A compromise was worked out which led eventually to the writing of a new rule.

HESE were times of great grief and trial for Francis, when he could see his initial poverty-inspired rule being diluted and fractured by an uncomprehending world. Francis decided to keep the fast that was held between August 15th, Mary's Assumption, and Saint Michæl's day, September 29th, on Mount La Verna. The year was 1224; he chose a handful of close friends that included his faithful companion, Brother Leo, to accompany him.

The event of the stigmata has been much pictured, and seems almost too awesome to approach. As he prayed on the morning of the feast of the cross immersed in The Passion of Christ, a flaming six-winged seraph in the form of the crucified appeared in the dawning sky. It approached rapidly, its pierced feet resting for a while on a rock. Then it was as if the seraph smote him in body and soul, and he was both in the greatest agony and the greatest joy. Mysteriously and in very truth he had shared in the death of Christ, for now he bore upon his hands, feet and side the very marks of his passion.

FRANCIS is not the only one to whom this great mystery has happened. Throughout church history there have been 300 men and women who bore the wounds of Christ, but he was the first. In mediæval times and perhaps still for a few today, it was possible to identify so strongly with the life, passion, death and resurrection of Christ that this could be a path of initiation.

Rudolf Steiner (1861-1925), the great spiritual investigator, describes this process. The monk, nun or hermit meditated very intensely on the seven steps of the Passion, beginning with the washing of the feet.

(I) In this exercise the aspirant imagines how everything higher bows down to the lower. The sacrifice of the lower is acknowledged. This meditation was eventually accompanied by the sensation of water swishing around the feet.

(II) In the scourging, the aspirant had to practise steadfastness despite the blows of fate. This meditation was accompanied by intense physical pain all over the body.

(III) In the crowning with thorns, the mockery of the world had to be borne, and physically an intense headache.

(IV) The fourth step was the bearing of the cross and the crucifixion. It was at this stage that the stigmata could occur.

(V) The crucifixion was followed by the so-called mystical death. Here the aspirant became aware of hell with its aspects of darkness and evil. He would experience the light of Christ pouring in the harrowing.

(VI) The sixth stage was an experience of burial, in which the body of the aspirant would extend throughout the very earth, as the body of Christ had done when it was entombed.

(VII) In the last and seventh stage, resurrection would be experienced. It was at this stage that the aspirant could truly say, "Not I but Christ in me." It is awesome to imagine that a human soul can be so purified that it can receive the very soul of Christ.

Francis lived for another two years after having received the wounds of the stigmata: a drawn-out Gethsemane, a burning spirit held within an ever-failing body. 'Brother Ass', as he called his body, was worn out. Frail and sick, suffering from the wounds of divine love, he travelled about on a donkey still teaching and inspiring.

The crypt beneath the Basilica of St Clare contains some touching relics, among them a fine undergarment and a pair of soft sandals made by Clare. He tried to hide his wounds, and his feet, bare to the naked earth, were now cushioned in protecting leather.

Towards the end he spent some time at the little convent of San Damiano. As a man he could not reside within its walls but was tended in a little bower made of branches in the sweet clean air of the herb garden. One can imagine that, despite his agony, this was a time of joy: a time when he and Clare could converse, be together, and find rejuvenation in their spiritual kinship. It was here in the little convent garden of San Damiano that the inspiration for his great canticle of the creatures came. The canticle was sung before Bishop Guido and the Mayor of Assisi who had quarrelled. The canticle worked like magic, and the two were reconciled, embracing each other. The canticle resounds like a mighty hymn through the ages:

MOST HIGH ALMIGHTY,
good Lord God, to Thee belong praise,
glory, honour and all blessing!

Praised be my Lord God with all His creatures,
and especially our Brother Sun, who brings us
the day and who brings us the light; fair is he
and shines with great splendour.
O Lord, he signifies to us Thee!

Praised be my Lord for our Sister Moon,
and for the stars, which He has set clear
and lovely in Heaven.

Praised be our Lord for our Brother Wind,
and for air and clouds, calms and all weather
by which Thou upholdest life in all creatures.

Praised be my Lord for our Sister Water, who is
very serviceable unto us and humble and
precious and clean.

Praised be my Lord for our Brother Fire, through
whom Thou givest us light in the darkness;
and he is bright and pleasant and very mighty and strong.

Praised be my Lord for our Mother Earth,
who sustains us and keeps us
and bringeth forth diverse fruits and flowers
of many colours and grass.

Praised be my Lord for all those who pardon
one another for love's sake and who endure
weakness and tribulation.

Blessed are they who peaceably shall endure,
For Thou, O most Highest, shalt give them a crown.

Praise ye and bless the Lord and give thanks unto Him
and serve Him with great humility.

ROTHER ELIAS, that strangely troubled soul, torn between love of Francis and ambition, was deeply worried about his health. He persuaded Francis to have the best treatment at the time, from Pope Honorius's own physicians. Mediæval (non-Arabic) medicine was crude and primitive in the extreme. His eye affliction, trachoma, caused him immense pain; his wasted body was attacked by malaria, a gastric ulcer, dyspepsia and swellings of the limbs. Added to this host of illnesses and suffering were the bleeding wounds of the stigmata. The papal doctors cauterised his eyes, they cut all the veins from his ears to his eyebrows, perforated both his ears, but to no effect.

Francis begged to be taken back to Assisi, and was carried by stretcher to Bishop Guido's palace. At one point in the journey, an armed contingent of crossbow men walked beside the stretcher to ensure that this living relic was not snatched away by Perugia.

The sentries on guard outside the palace must have been amazed to hear so much singing pouring from the bedchamber of the dying man. When his terrible pains reached an almost unbearable pitch, he seemed to become ever more fully a singing voice of worship. It was probably at this point that the last verse of his canticle to the creatures was composed:

> "Praised be my Lord for our sister, the death
> of the body, from which no man escapeth.
> Woe to him who dies in mortal sin!
> Blessed are they who are found walking by
> Thy most holy will, for the second death
> shall have no power to do them harm."

After a time in Assisi, his wish to end his life in the Portiuncula, where his mission had begun, was granted. He sent letters of farewell to Clare and her nuns. The Roman noblewoman, Jacqueline of Settesoli, who is considered the mother of the Franciscan Third Order, arrived just in time. She brought with her an ash-coloured shroud that she had made for his burial, candles and some almond cakes. It had been revealed to her in a dream that the dying man wished for them. Francis tasted the cakes and blessed her. He died on October 3rd 1226, intoning with his last breath a versicle from a psalm:

> "Free my soul from prison so that
> I may praise Thy name."

At the instant of his death, a great flock of skylarks rose above the roof.

The Plates

BROTHER SUN

"PRAISED *be my Lord God with all His creatures, and especially our Brother Sun who brings us the day and who brings us the light. Fair is he and shines with great splendour. O Lord, he signifies to us Thee."*

St Francis

size 60 x 30 inches
oil on wood

THE DRAPER'S SHOP

PIETRO BERNARDONE *was a wealthy cloth merchant with a shop near 'Piazza del Comune'. He imported beautiful fabrics from France, including velvets, furs, damasks and embroidered samite. It was here that Francis started his apprenticeship in the family business when he was fourteen.*

One day a beggar entered the shop and asked him for alms "in the name of Christ". Francis angrily sent him away with nothing, but later he felt remorse for what he had done, and vowed never again to refuse anyone who asked him for help "in the name of Christ".

size 14 x 16 inches
woodcut print on paper

St Francis • The Draper shop •

THE POOR TABLE

WHILE *Pietro Bernadone was away from home on his travels, the young Francis took the opportunity to invite a crowd of poor people to eat at his home. He began to lay the table with food for a large number. When his mother Pica asked him what he was doing, he said it was "for the poor". His mother, who loved Francis, accepted this kindness and marvelled greatly in her heart.*

size 38¼ x 16 inches
tempera on wood

THE TRIPUDIANTI

AS a young man Francis became part of the Tripudianti, a group of wealthy young men who spent their time merrymaking, banqueting and entertaining beautiful young women, in the style of the early troubadours. Down the narrow streets of Assisi they would come singing and dancing, torches aflame, with instruments playing. Heading the riotous Tripudianti would be Francis, the 'King of Feasts'.

size 25 x 18¼ inches
woodcut print

FRANCIS OF ASSISI 36

St Francis
1182
of ASSISI
1226

FRANCIS MEETS THE LEPER

DRESSED *as the son of a wealthy merchant, Francis was riding on a horse past San Lazzaro leper hospital near Assisi. He saw with horror a disfigured leper with bloodstained sores standing in his path. He dismounted from his horse. As if drawn by a power he could not resist, he walked over to the leper and pressed a gold coin into his hand. Then, moved by deep compassion, he embraced the leper, kissing him on both cheeks. As his gaze fell to the ground a great flood of emotion filled his whole being. When Francis looked up, the leper was no longer there. He had vanished. He realised he had met his brother in Christ. His whole world seemed transformed, and a courageous compassion filled him from that moment onwards.*

size 48 x 36 inches
tempera on canvas

THE DREAM

FRANCIS *had a wonderful dream that he was in a palace filled with shining armour; shields and spears surrounded him, marked with the cross of Christ. He thought the armour was for him and his knights, and soon he would become a mighty prince going bravely into battle. He soon realised his path in life was to be different, to be a knight of God, needing great courage to face the moral darkness of his age.*

size 22½ x 19¾ inches
tempera on wood

THE ILLNESS

A YEAR *after Francis was taken prisoner at Perugia, he returned to Assisi in the spring of 1204. He was twenty-two years old. Shortly after this he became seriously ill with a high fever, and nearly died. This was an inner crucifixion which changed his life. The valiant knight of his dream was transformed into a man who had now forged spiritual weapons of mercy, compassion and love. The moral impulses of his inner life could now work into the world in a Christ-like way.*

size 23¼ x 15¼ inches
tempera & mixed media on wood

THE REVELATION

IN THE *small church of San Damiano, Francis knelt and prayed. Looking up towards the crucifix, he heard the words of Christ:*

"Go, Francis, and repair my house, which is falling into ruin."

size 17½ x 21 inches
tempera on wood

THE BEATING

FRANCIS, *having sold his father's valuable cloth to rebuild the church, was given a cruel flogging by Pietro Bernadone and flung into a small underground room. There Francis stayed for a few days alone, in near darkness. His father had hoped this would bring him to his senses, but it only strengthened his resolve to follow the suffering of Christ. His mother Pica let him out while his father was away.*

size 15½ x 11¾ inches
wax & watercolour on paper

St Francis

THE TRIAL

A GREAT *crowd gathered by Piazza Vescovada, the tree-lined square by the Romanesque church of Santa Maria Maggiore. It was here in front of the Bishop's palace in 1207 that St Francis was brought to trial by his angry father, to face Bishop Guido and the people of Assisi.*

In a dramatic gesture, St Francis gave back all his clothes and gold to his father, saying: "Until this day I have called Pietro Bernardone my father, but from now on I can say without reserve, 'Our Father which art in heaven'."

size 48 x 24 inches
tempera & mixed media on wood

FRANCIS & LADY POVERTY

FRANCIS *turned his back on the crowd at the Bishop's palace, and wandered through the orchard with his 'bride' Lady Poverty. Francis was given a rough, ragged shirt to wear by a friendly gardener. He drew with chalk a large cross on the back of it. Leaving Assisi behind, with the night coming on, he walked northwards towards Gubbio through the moonlit mountains. Francis and his bride were guided mysteriously onward as if they had entered a silvery Eden landscape, beckoned by the golden fruit of destiny on the tree of life.*

size 29 x 36 inches.
tempera & mixed media on sacking

FRANCIS AT GUBBIO LEPER HOUSE

Francis helped for a while in the Leper House in the town of Gubbio on the slopes of Monte Calvo.

size 16½ x 12 inches
sepia ink & wax on paper

ST Francis

THE PORTIUNCULA

THE *small church of the Portiuncula lies just below Assisi, in the plain of Umbria. Its origins go back many centuries. According to the legend Francis loved, four pilgrims had come back from the Holy Land in the fourth century and had founded the church. They had sanctified the ancient shrine with a precious relic that they had carried back with them. They sang praises to God there.*

In later years, visiting hermits, peasants and small children who gathered flowers, had heard angels singing there. And so the place came to be called 'Santa Maria degli Angeli'. Later, Benedictine Monks lived there for six hundred years. When Francis came, the monastery ruins were still there hidden in the woods, deserted for nearly a hundred years, left to the birds and the angels. Francis rebuilt the church, which was to become the founding mother church for the Order.

size 32 x 16 inches
tempera & oil on wood

BROTHER HORSE

"He called all creatures brother...he discerned the hidden things of nature with his sensitive heart."

Thomas of Celano

size 33 x 27 inches
tempera & mixed media on sacking

ST FRANCIS & THE DOVE

"The Peace of God be with you."

St Francis

size 48 x 22 inches
tempera on canvas

ST CLARE

ST CLARE *was a beautiful daughter of Assisian nobility, who had given up all her inheritance to follow St Francis, to live a life of poverty. Her hair was cut short and her clothes were simple; she became a spiritual companion to St Francis, and set up the order of 'Poor Clares' in the small church of San Damiano. Living alone with the 'Poor Clares', her life was one of devotion to God, chastity and self-denial. They all worked hard together with regular hours and nurtured a herb garden with flowers.*

size 41 x 22½ inches
tempera & silver on wood

ST CLARE

Clare had a bright clarity in her eyes, and she would sing with the 'Poor Clares' in the small choir room at the back of the chapel.

size 35 x 25 x 4 inches
yellow guiting stone

FRANCIS & THE TURTLE DOVES

APPEARING *in the early morning mist was a boy from the town of Siena. He had caught a number of turtle doves in a snare, and was carrying them to market to sell. Francis, upon seeing the doves, said "Good boy, please give me the doves so that such innocent birds, which in holy scripture are symbols of pure, humble and faithful souls, will not fall into the hands of cruel men who will kill them."*

The boy gave the doves to Francis, who held them close and talked to them in a very gentle way. He made nests for them, and the doves soon settled and laid eggs, rearing their young among the Friars. The boy later joined the order of Franciscans.

size 36 x 36 inches
tempera on canvas

PREACHING AT SAN RUFINO SQUARE

PEOPLE *gathered from all around Assisi to hear St Francis preach. His strong resonant voice would ring out across the square as he greeted the people, saying: "The Lord give thee peace." He spoke eloquently, in a simple, sincere way that could reach the heart of each individual. When he was moved by the Spirit, enraptured by his praises for God, he gesticulated with his hands, and his feet would spring up and down.*

The universe seemed nearer as he spoke, as if Francis could almost reach out his hand and touch the stars, Brother Sun and Sister Moon. The angels surrounded all he did.

size 15 x 11½ inches
sepia & watercolour on paper

ST Francis

BROTHER FISH

THE *boat gently rocks on Lake Rieti, while Francis sits silently in prayer. He listens to the angel as the silver grey light of the moon falls over his sackcloth tunic and the waters.*

A local fisherman kindly gives him a large fish. He joyfully calls it brother, then places it back in the water, praising the Lord. He continues in prayer for some time while the fish merrily plays, waiting for him to finish. Francis now kindly gives him leave to go.

size 34 x 31 inches
tempera & silver on wood

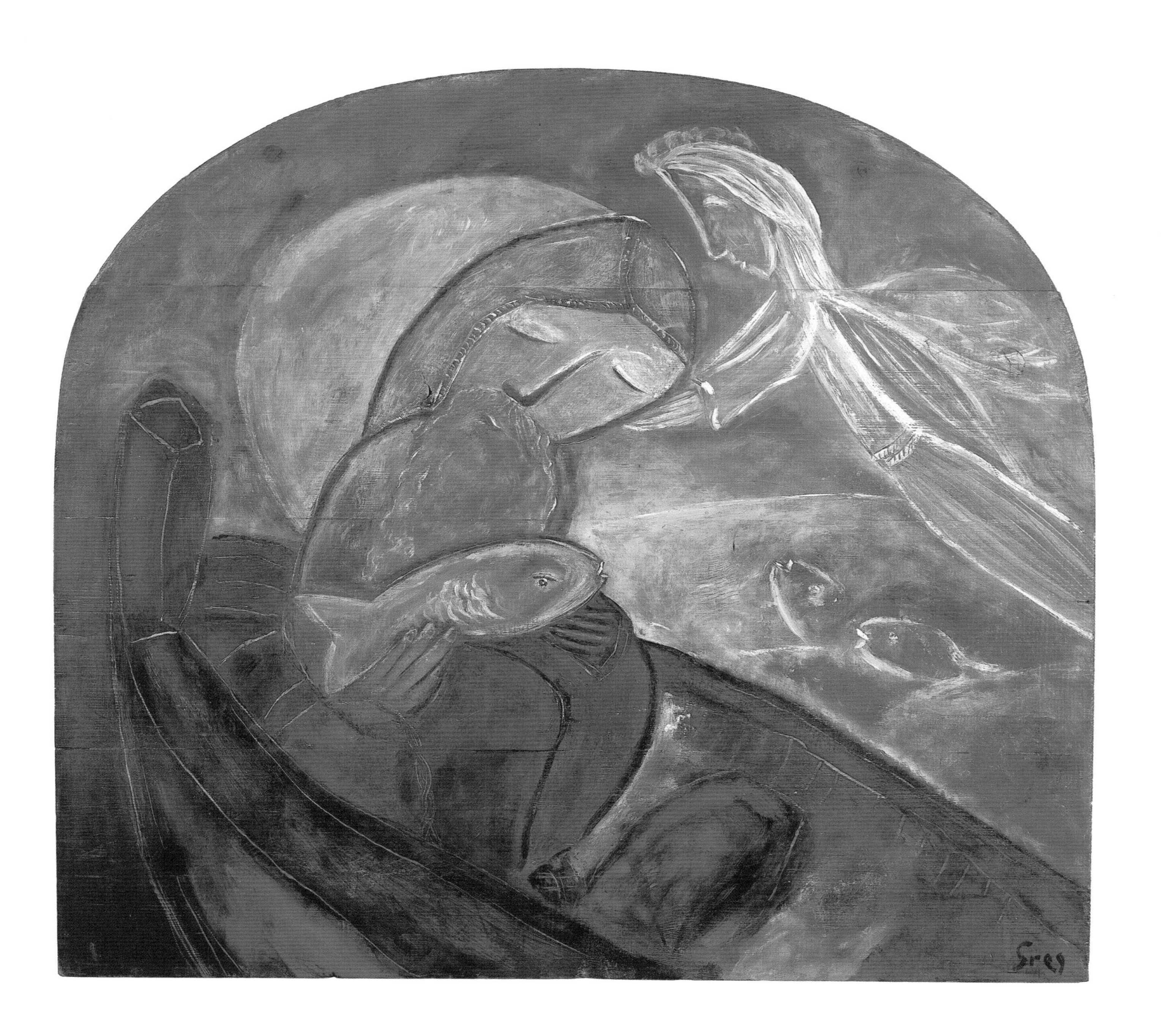

JOHN THE RUSTIC

WHEN *Francis was in Nottiano, a small village east of Assisi, he found a church not as clean as he would like. He felt that churches and altars should be looked after with careful reverence. He often carried a broom and set to work cleaning the church. Nearby a ploughman called John, 'a rustic of strange simplicity', left his plough and oxen in the fields and went to find St Francis.*

While St Francis dusted the stone flag steps John said: "Give me the broom, for I wish to help thee." This Francis did, and they spent time working and talking together about God and the 'Order'. John later joined the 'Order of Friars Minor'. The condition for those joining the Order was that they give away all their possessions to the poor. So John the rustic gave away his ox to the poor. His parents were most upset about this, until they realised St Francis had asked for the ox to be given to them.

size 15 x 12 inches
sepia ink & chalk on paper

Greg

ST FRANCIS PREACHES TO THE BIRDS

FRANCIS *came to a place near Bevagna where many birds had congregated. Greeting them in his usual way, he was filled with great joy and said:*

"My brothers, you should praise your creator very much and always love him; he gave you feathers to clothe you, wings so you can fly and whatever else was necessary for you. God made you noble among his creatures and he gave you a home in the pure air; though you neither sow nor reap, he nevertheless protects and governs you without any anxiety on your part." After hearing these words, the birds rejoiced in a wonderful way.

size 16½ x 16½ inches
Portland limestone

CARCERI HERMITAGE

GOING *over Mount Subasio from Assisi, a rocky path leads to a steep ravine cut into the mountainside. High up in the ravine are small caves nestled into the woods, called by St Francis 'The Carceri'. It was here that the 'Friars Minor' would fast and pray. In the spring, cyclamen flowers covered the ground, and wild dog roses grew on the banks. It was here St Francis held a singing contest with a nightingale, which the nightingale won. It wasn't all roses; for in winter time of sleet, rain, and snow, a torrent of water could rush down the ravine. Then the friars' beds of straw covered with rags became damp and wet.*

At the ravine summit lies a humble XII-century Mary chapel with faded walls, that overlooks the valley below. Under this chapel a narrow passage winds downwards over stone steps into the 'grotto', where St Francis would stay in solitude. There is a small window here that overlooks the sheer drop of the ravine valley. When it was opened, St Francis could see the white doves flying in the early morning light, like Noah opening the latch of the Ark after a damp, dark journey of the soul.

size 19¾ x 19¾ inches
tempera & oil on wood

ST FRANCIS WITH THE LEPER

Our brother in Christ

size 26 x 17 inches
tempera & pencil on wood

ST FRANCIS IN THE SNOW

"Poverty is to have nothing, to wish for nothing, yet to possess all things truly in the spirit of freedom."

St Francis

size 29½ x 31½ inches
tempera & mixed media on canvas

SANTA MARIA DEGLI ANGELI

AS *well as leading a simple life of prayer and poverty, the 'Friars Minor' were encouraged by Francis to work hard in the fields, to craft their own livelihoods and make small shelters of reeds, wattle and mud.*

The small church of Santa Maria degli Angeli was greatly loved by St Francis, for it signified their poor, humble beginnings, a closeness to the angels and to Mary the mother of Christ.

size 15¼ x 12 inches
watercolour & sepia on paper

Greg
Santa Maria Degli Angeli
ST FRANCIS
PORZIUNCOLA
ASSISI

MEETING THE POPE

FRANCIS *and his twelve Friars journeyed on foot to Rome to seek confirmation of their Order. St Francis and the ragged sackclothed Friars filed into the rich Papal court to appear before Pope Innocent III. He sat in his great chair, with the cardinals grouped around him in their gorgeous robes. Francis kneeled, arms outstretched, and spoke with loving reverence of Christ, and how they were following the life of poverty, as exemplified in the Gospels.*

When he asked for the Order to be confirmed, the Pope said: "My son, go and pray to Jesus that he may show us his will." This Francis did, and the will of God was revealed to him in the form of a parable, and to the Pope in a dream. The Pope confirmed the Order, and the Friars walked back towards Assisi rejoicing and singing praises.

size 21 x 17¾ inches
sepia, watercolour & wax on paper

MINSTRELS OF GOD

HAVING *composed the 'Canticle of Brother Sun', St Francis felt inspired to create a melody in music to complement the words of his poem. He then sent the 'Friars Minor' out like mediæval travelling minstrels to sing the Canticle in various towns. He said they were to form a circle together in the market place, and one of them was to preach a sermon. Afterwards the Friars were to sing the Canticle of Brother Sun, and then one of them should say: "We are the wandering minstrels of God, and the only reward we ask is that you lead a life of true penitence."*

size 37 x 48 inches
tempera & mixed media on wood

THE SHARED BOWL

A LEPER *who was ill and suffering was being cared for by Brother James, a simple-hearted childlike person. He thought it would be a nice change for the leper to leave the hospital and to walk through the oak wood towards the Portiuncula. They set out, meeting St Francis on the way, who was horrified and said: "You must not lead these Brother Christians abroad in this fashion; it is not decent for you or them." But as soon as he had spoken, he regretted it, realising how much his words could hurt the leper. To show his penance, St Francis said: "I will eat out of the same bowl as my Brother Christian." So a bowl of food was placed between them. His fingers touched the leper's fingers as they ate together from the same bowl. Francis was ready to lose his life rather than to be unkind.*

size 14 x 14 inches
sepia ink & chalk on paper

ST Francis
sreg

THE SUFFERING

St Francis could never forget the Sufferings of Christ,
and his longing to share them consumed him.

size 13½ x 10¼ inches
sepia ink, watercolour & wax on paper

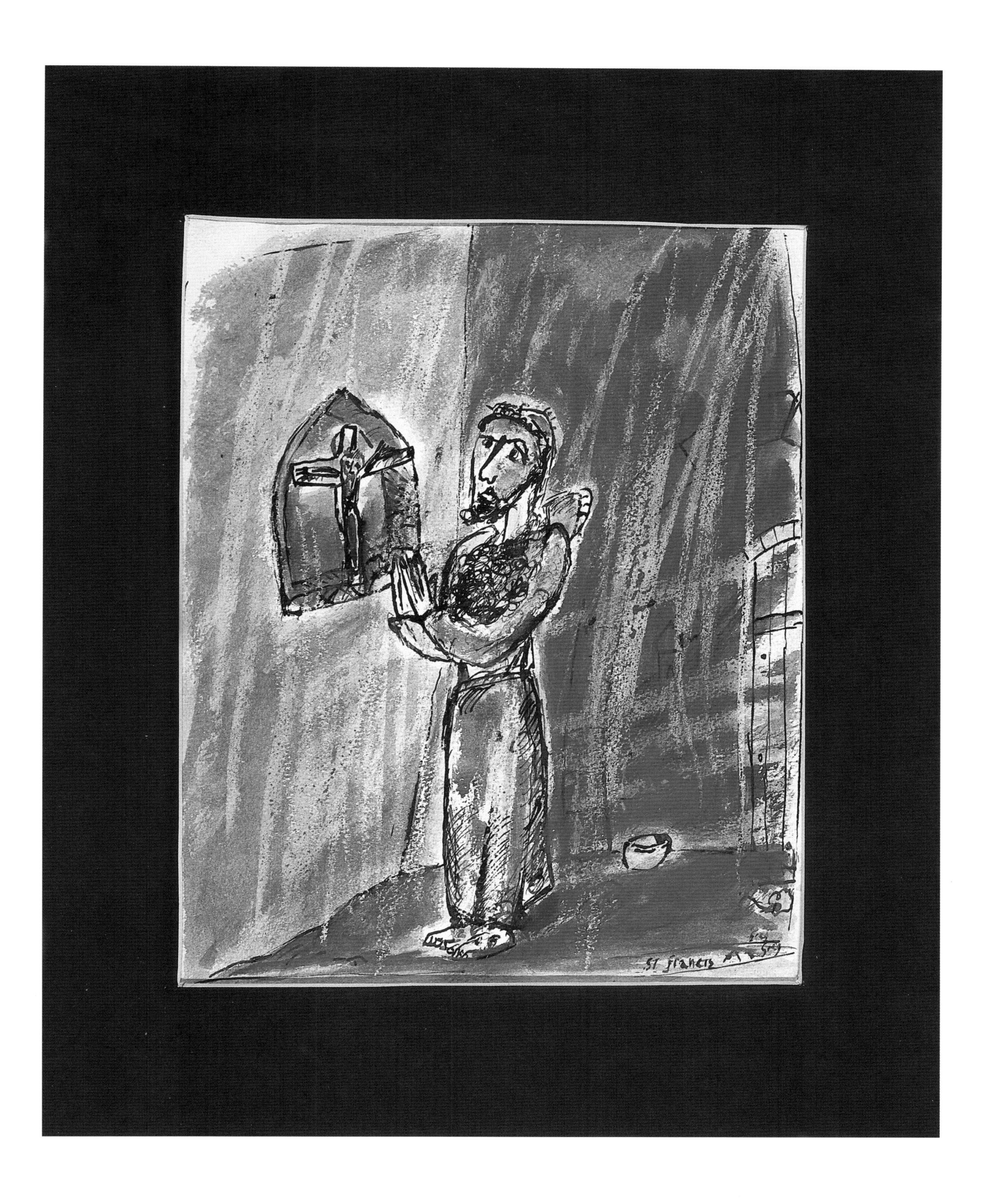
St francis

ST FRANCIS WITH SISTER BIRD

size 84 x 23½ inches
Tetbury shelly limestone

FRANCIS PRAYS IN SAN DAMIANO

"All highest glorious God, cast your light into the darkness of my heart. Give me right faith, firm hope, perfect charity and profound humility, with wisdom and perfection, O Lord, so that I may do what is your most holy will."

St Francis

size 8½ x 6 inches
line drawing

St Francis.
ST DAmiano
Greg

FRIAR RUFFINO

BEFORE *joining the Order, Friar Ruffino was an aristocrat of Assisi, of the noble family of the Scefi. He was a shy, lonely man, who had a lifelong battle to overcome his fears and anxieties. When he joined the Order he became a dedicated man of prayer. Yet he shied away from speaking in public places. As a 'Brother Minor' he had pledged to preach the gospel, and so Francis told him to go and preach in Assisi, and be done with it!*

Ruffino said he could not go. St Francis then lost his temper, and ordered him as a 'Brother Minor' to take off his outer tunic and, wearing only his breeches, to go and preach in Assisi. He reluctantly obeyed, and set off through the streets. People jeered at him as he went towards the pulpit to preach by the Cathedral. Meanwhile, Francis was feeling deep remorse for having given such a harsh order to the sensitive friar, a nobleman of Assisi. He felt that as a penance he should suffer the same fate, so he also threw off his tunic and walked into Assisi with only his breeches on. Entering the square, he waited until Ruffino's sermon stumbled to an end. Francis then mounted the pulpit and stood next to him, as the crowd roared even more with laughter. But the laughter died away as Francis talked to them of poverty, nakedness and the suffering of Christ. The crowd became moved by his words, and were changed in their hearts by his preaching.

size 16½ x 12 inches
sepia, watercolour and wax on paper

Frior Rufino
St Francis
Greg 2003

THE TEMPTATION

ST FRANCIS *was seeking at all times to follow the will of God in his life. He was often tormented by demons and temptations; they would fight with the angels of light on the battleground of his own inner self.*

size 14 x 10 inches
sepia ink & watercolour on paper

BROTHER CROW

THERE *is something humorous about Brother Crow, even though he is black and could be seen as frightening. He became a good friend to St Francis. He went to the choir with the Brothers, ate with them in the refectory, and visited the sick in the infirmary of the friary. He even went with the Brothers to the houses of Assisi to beg for alms. When St Francis died, it is said that Brother Crow refused to leave his tomb and died there from grief and weakness.*

size 30 x 40 inches
tempera, charcoal & pastel on canvas

THE BASKET

ST FRANCIS *was walking along the road that runs from Todi to Perugia when he passed a woman with a basket on her head. Intuitively he knew something was wrong, so he stopped the woman and asked her: "Where are you going?" She said, "To the river to wash these clothes of mine." St Francis said: "Nay woman, what you carry belongs to God. Set down the basket and I will take care of him." She put the basket down and Francis lifted away the dirty linen and took in his arms a newborn baby which she had intended to drown in the river. Francis entrusted the child to be cared for by a charitable woman. Later he built a small house on the place where the baby was saved. This became a foundling hospital for illegitimate children of the poor.*

size 13½ x 10¾ inches
sepia ink & watercolour on paper

ST Francis

THE LEPER HOUSE

IN *a Leper House there was a man deeply ill in body and soul, who even blasphemed the Mother of Christ. Although the Friars were patient and tried to help the man, he heaped insults upon them, as one possessed of a devil. So they went to seek the help of St Francis. He came and said: "God give thee peace, my brother." The leper answered: "What peace can I have from God who hath taken peace from me and made me all rotten and stinking?"*

Francis prayed to God for help. Then he boiled water with many sweet herbs and washed the leper's sores, while another Friar poured water over him. With angelic help and the healing hands of St Francis, the leprosy departed miraculously. Both in body and mind the man became whole.

size 13½ x 9½ inches.
sepia ink & chalk on paper

FRANCIS WITH VIOL

Francis was a joyful man, who in fun would draw a stick across his arm as if he played a viol, and sing French praises.

"Who indeed are God's servants, if not minstrels who seek to move men's hearts in order to lead them into the joys of the spirit?"

St Francis

size 11 x 13 inches
oil on wood

BROTHER BEE

THE *humming of Brother Bee is heard in the garden. His wings move miraculously as he flies over the hexagon honeycombs and comes to rest on the hand of St Francis, who dearly loves him.*

size 5¾ x 9¼ inches
sepia ink & watercolour on paper

ST. Francis c Bee
Greg

BROTHER WOLF

WHILE *staying in the mountain town of Gubbio, St Francis heard that nearby a large fierce wolf was roving around, devouring animals and attacking people.*

The people of Gubbio were so terrified that no-one dared go outside the city gate. St Francis went out bravely to meet the wolf, placing his faith in Christ. In sight of many people the fierce wolf came running at him. He made the sign of the Cross and said: "Come to me, Brother Wolf; in the name of Christ I order you not to harm me or anyone." The wolf slowed down and lay at the feet of St Francis. St Francis asked him to make a pledge not to hurt the people of Gubbio again. The wolf agreed by placing his paw into his hand.

size 15½ x 11½ inches
sepia ink & watercolour on paper

St Francis & the Wolf

ST FRANCIS IN THE MARSHES

ST FRANCIS *was walking with another Friar in the Venetian marshes when he came upon a large flock of birds singing among the reeds. When he saw them he said: "Our sisters the birds are praising their creator. We will go in among them and sing God's praises chanting the divine office."*

But with the birds singing so loudly, the Friars could not hear themselves singing. St Francis said to the birds: "My sisters, stop singing until we have given God the praise to which he has the right." The birds were silent as they listened to the Friars singing their praises, and then they started to sing joyfully.

size 60 x 60 inches
tempera & mixed media on wood

THE CHARIOT

ONE NIGHT *the Brothers were praying at Rivo-Torto when a radiant light suddenly brightened the dark hovel where they were staying. Looking up into the sky, they saw St Francis racing across the sky in a fiery chariot, like Elijah in a ball of brightness. The Brothers knew that St Francis was staying in a house far away, yet this was a sign that he was with them in spirit and prayer. A light seemed to illuminate the hidden souls of the Brothers so that they could see into the innermost self of each other.*

size 13 x 11 inches
watercolour & sepia ink on paper

FRIARS IN OXFORD

THE *Friars Minor came to England in September 1224; a grey cold land, very distant from their sunny Italy. Having landed, they travelled through London and Canterbury and arrived in Oxford. On Christmas Day it was bitterly cold as they walked through a wood nearby the town. The snow and mud were frozen to the ground as the two friars followed a rough path with their naked feet.*

Maybe thinking of their beloved 'Portiuncula' far away, where the other friars would joyously be singing at Santa Maria degli Angeli, the younger friar suddenly said: "Father, shall I sing to lighten your journey?" Then he thundered forth a 'Salve Regina Misericordiæ'. When the hymn was finished, he said with a kind of self-congratulation, "Brother, was not that antiphonal well sung?"

size 15½ x 11½ inches
sepia ink & watercolour on paper

Greg
Friers Oxford
of St Francis

BROTHER JUNIPER

BROTHER JUNIPER *was the beloved jester of the Order from their earliest beginnings. He was simple-hearted and St Francis loved him so much that he said "he wished he had a forest of such junipers." After the death of St Francis, the Order numbered thousands, convents were built and administered by 'superiors'. Absolute poverty was no longer possible in the way Friar Juniper had been taught by St Francis. Following the original rule, he would regularly give away his clothes, books or church ornaments to the poor. On one occasion he even cut off some sumptuously adorned 'silver bells of great worth' from a gold hanging on a church altar and gave them to a poor woman, saying: "These bells are a superfluity." The superior berated Friar Juniper very severely for this and raised his voice so high that he got hoarse with a sore throat.*

Thinking nothing for himself, Friar Juniper went to the city to beg for butter and flour to make a 'pottage' to help the superior's sore throat. Very late in the night, the superior heard a knock at his door. Feeling exhausted, he opened the door to Friar Juniper, who held a candle in one hand and the bowl of hot pottage in the other. Juniper smiled in his childlike way and said: "My father, as your voice is sore I have made a mess of pottage for thee." For the superior, the late interruption of his sleep was the last straw. He lost his temper again and told him to go away. But Juniper stood there full of pity and love, holding out the bowl. But it was not accepted. Simple Juniper did not want the pottage to be wasted, so he said: "If you will not eat, my father, I pray thee do this for me: hold the candle and I myself will eat it." The superior broke down, and took Juniper into his cell where they ate the pottage together.

size 17 x 12 inches
watercolour, wax & sepia ink on paper

MEETING THE DEMONS

WHILE *St Francis was walking in the Spoleto valley he found an abandoned church. He went in to pray, and being tired, he fell asleep. Not sleeping well, he awoke in the dark, lonely church knowing he was surrounded by evil, and he felt terrified. Angels and demons were very real to Francis, and he felt he was being attacked by demons. Battling in his mind and body, he overcame his fear and faced the darker forces through prayer. He prayed to Christ; then going outside the church he crossed himself, calling to God under the stars. He then felt at peace.*

size 14 x 10 inches
sepia ink & watercolour on paper

Greg
St. francis

BROTHER LAMB

W HILE *in Rome, St Francis had a lamb which he kept out of reverence for Christ the 'Lamb of God'. He loved the lamb's humble, gentle nature. The lamb would stay with him, wake up with him and sometimes walk with him to church.*

size 18 x 9½ inches
chalk, pencil & sepia on wood

Greg
ST Francis & The Lamb

DRAGGED THROUGH THE STREET

RECOVERING *from a severe fever, St Francis had allowed himself to eat a meal of broth made with meat. This helped him recover from his illness, but he felt he had strayed from his life of poverty and strict abstinence. As a penance, he ordered Friar Peter to drag him through the street tied to a rope, almost naked. It was winter time with frost on the ground as Francis was dragged into the square. He ordered a friar to throw a bowl of ash over him and said to the gathered crowd: "I confess to God and to you, I have eaten in my infirmity broth made of flesh."*

size 19½ x 17 inches
sepia ink & watercolour on paper

2003
St Francis

ST FRANCIS IN THE RAIN

WHILE *on a journey, nearing the end of his life, Francis was riding through the countryside. He suddenly stopped his horse, and dismounted. He threw back his hood and kneeled in the pouring rain, praying with great devotion and reverence. It was the hour of the day when he said his prayers, whatever the situation.*

size 14¼ x 11¼ inches
sepia ink & wax on paper

THE PARALYSED BOY

AT *Tuscannella a little boy was lying paralysed in his bed. Francis went up to the room where he stayed. He prayed in the name of Christ, and blessed the boy. Then he lifted him up in his arms, and set him on the ground. In the sight of all the people, the boy rose up and began to walk.*

size 16½ x 11½ inches
watercolour, sepia ink & wax on paper

Greg
S.T. Francis & the Boy

THE FAST ON LAKE PERUGIA

Alone on a small island on Lake Perugia, St Francis fasted for forty days with only two small loaves of bread.

"Lord make me an instrument of thy peace."

St Francis

size 38 x 22 inches
tempera on wood

SISTER DRAGONFLY

SISTER *Dragonfly swiftly moves across the water, over wild grasses, white daisies and cornflowers, then rests for a moment with her beautiful fine wings on the hand of St Francis.*

size 8½ x 5¾ inches
line drawing

Greg
ST Francis & Dragon Fly

THE MIRACLE SPRING

WHILE *St Francis and the brothers were climbing Mount La Verna, a kindly peasant gave St Francis a donkey to ride on, and walked along beside them. Later, while going up the steep mountain path in the summer heat, the peasant called out to St Francis: "I am dying of thirst." St Francis got off the donkey and began to pray. He kneeled on the ground, his hands raised towards heaven, and prayed until he knew God had answered him. He then said to the peasant: "Run quickly to that rock, and there you will find running water which Christ in his mercy has just caused to flow from the rock." The peasant found the spring water flowing through the hard rock and drank.*

size 14½ x 11½ inches
watercolour on paper

ST Francis

ST FRANCIS ON MOUNT LA VERNA

ST FRANCIS *fasted and prayed for many days in a little cell on the summit of Mount La Verna. Having been in deep contemplation, he looked towards the heavens from the edge of the world. He saw a seraph with six flaming wings appearing swiftly from the sky. As the seraph came nearer, he could feel the presence of the crucified Christ. St Francis received the holy stigmata imprinted into his hands, feet and side with pain and joy.*

The whole of Mount La Verna seemed to light up in flames, illuminating the mountains, followed by sounds of thunder. Far below in the valley the shepherds with their flocks were gripped in fear.

size 50 x 30 inches
tempera & silver on canvas

FRANCIS OF ASSISI 134

CHRIST

The Passion of Christ

size 15 x 13 inches
oil on wood

Grey

THE BLESSING

NEARLY *blind and very weak, St Francis was carried by the Friars down the slopes of Assisi back to the Portiuncula, where he wished to end his days. Passing through the countryside, he asked them to stop and turn him around so that he could face Assisi. Raising himself up on the bed, he gazed for the last time on the walls of Assisi that he had helped rebuild, on the terraces he played in as a child, and on the tiled roofs climbing up the mountainside.*

Then he raised his hand and blessed the city and the people, saying: "Blessed be thou of the Lord, holy city faithful to God, for through thee shall many souls be saved and in thee shall dwell many servants of the most high, and from thee shall many be chosen for the eternal kingdom."

size 13¼ x 11¼ inches
sepia ink & chalk on canvas

THE PASSING OF ST FRANCIS

ST FRANCIS *passed away at the Portiuncula, the humble place that he loved, of Santa Maria degli Angeli. People from all walks of life came to see him. Early next morning the Brothers carried him on a bier as they sang, with candles aglow, passing over palm branches. Trumpets sounded as the procession of people from Assisi and the Friars made their way slowly up the hill from the Portiuncula.*

They were going to the church of San Giorgio, where he was to be laid to rest. It was also there he first went to school, and later gave his first sermon as a Friar Minor. On the way, they stopped at the church of San Damiano. The brothers carried the bier with St Francis's body into the chapel. They went over to the grille (partition) where St Clare and her Sisters were waiting. They moved the iron grating and held the bier up in their arms, so she could see him. St Clare looked for the last time on the peaceful, ashen face of St Francis.

size 27½ x 24 inches
tempera & mixed media on wood

Bibliography

Saint Francis of Assisi
by Elizabeth Goudge
Gerald Duckworth & Co., London

The Little Flowers of Saint Francis
The Mirror of Perfection by Leo of Assisi
The Life of St Francis by St. Bonaventura
Introduction by Thomas Okey
Everyman Library, J. M. Dent & Sons Ltd, London

The Spiritual Foundation of Morality
by Rudolf Steiner
Steiner Book Centre, Canada
ISBN 0 919924 09 3

Giotto: The Legend of St Francis in the Assisi Basilica
by Bruno Dozzini
Editrice Minerva Assisi
ISBN 88 87021 47 3

The Life of St Francis of Assisi and *The Treatise of Miracles*
by Thomas of Celano
Editrice Minerva Assisi
ISBN 88 87021 06 6

The Writings of St Francis translated by Ignatius Brady O.F.M.
Casa Editrice Francescana Assisi
Edizioni Porziuncola

Esoteric Christianity and the Mission of Christian Rosenkreutz
Rudolf Steiner Press
ISBN 0 85 440 413 7

The Life and Times of St Francis
Paul Hamlyn
(Portraits of Greatness Series)

Man on the Threshold
by Bernard Lievegoed
Hawthorn Press, Gloucester
ISBN 0 950706 26 4

Francis of Assisi
Canticle of Creatures
by Paul M. Allen and Joan De Ris Allen
Floris Books
ISBN 0 86 315 242 2